MW01097925

A SINGLE SHARD

by
Linda Sue Park

Teacher Guide

Written by
Debbie Triska Keiser

Edited by
Katherine E. Martinez

> ### Note
> The Clarion Books hardcover edition of the book, published by Houghton Mifflin ©2001, was used to prepare this guide. The page references may differ in other editions.
>
> **Please note:** Please assess the appropriateness of this book for the age level and maturity of your students prior to reading and discussing it with your class.

ISBN 1-58130-770-5

To order, contact your local school supply store, or—

Novel Units, Inc.
P.O. Box 97
Bulverde, TX 78163-0097

Web site: www.educyberstor.com

Table of Contents

Skills and Strategies

Writing
    Personal writing, character
    journal, creative writing,
    poetry, reports, essays, skits

Literary Elements
    Literary analysis, story
    mapping, plot development,
    setting, character analysis

Across the Curriculum
    Social Studies—developing
    maps, research; Science—
    climate, ages of trees,
    inventions, biology; Math—
    symmetry; Art—designing
    maps, illustrations, making
    models, collages; Health—diet

Listening/Speaking
    Storytelling, discussion, oral
    reports, interviewing, skits

Thinking
    Identifying attributes,
    research, brainstorming,
    problem solving, creative
    thinking, critical thinking,
    compare/contrast, decision
    making

Comprehension
    Predicting, facts and details,
    sequencing, foreshadowing,
    cause/effect, inference,
    context clues, summarizing,
    drawing conclusions

Vocabulary
    Pictionary, word maps,
    synonyms, antonyms,
    defining, parts of speech,
    context clues

Genre: fiction

Setting: 12th-century Korea

Point of View: third-person narrative

Themes: survival, pride, persistence, patience

Conflict: man vs. man, man vs. himself, man vs. nature

Style: third-person narrative

Tone: optimistic

Date of First Publication: 2001

Summary

Tree-ear is a young orphan who yearns to throw a celadon pot on a potter's wheel. He lives with his friend Crane-man under a bridge and they scavenge for everything they have. Tree-ear begins working for the potter, Min, in order to pay a debt. While Tree-ear is away on business for the potter, Crane-man is killed. When Tree-ear returns with a commission for Min, he is asked to stay with the potter and his wife and to learn the trade of pottery.

Background Information

The idea for *A Single Shard* came from a piece of Korean celadon pottery dated back to the 12th century. The vase is inlaid with cranes encircled in medallions and is considered a cultural treasure in Korea.

About the Author

Linda Sue Park, the daughter of Korean immigrants, was born and raised in Illinois. She has written short stories and poetry all of her life. She has a degree in English from Stanford University and has worked in education, advertising, and the oil business. She has published three other novels, many poems, and short stories. This book, *A Single Shard*, is the 2002 Newbery Medal winner.

Introductory Activities

1. Previewing the Book: Have students study the cover and consider the title. Then ask students to read and discuss the Acknowledgements. Based on their discussion, students predict what the book will be about.

2. Research: Have students research Linda Sue Park on the Internet.

3. Predict: Given the following clues, have students write a paragraph predicting what they think will happen in the story:

   orphan　　　　pottery　　　　travel　　　　robbery　　　　death　　　　apprentice

4. Character Journal: List the main characters from *A Single Shard* and ask students to select one. As students read the book, encourage students to keep a journal of the character's thoughts and actions from that character's point of view. Invite students to share their journal entries with classmates periodically.

5. Prediction Chart: Have students set up a prediction chart (see pages 7-8 of this guide) to use as they read the book.

6. Attribute Web: Create an attribute web (page 9 of this guide) with students for each of the following ideas: persistence, bravery, friendship, acceptance. Ask students to brainstorm what each word brings to mind. Encourage students to elaborate on their particular ideas. Ask students to predict how each idea will be brought to light in the book.

7. Freewriting: Give students the following prompts. Ask them to choose one and freewrite about it for at least ten minutes.

   • How would life be different for you if you lived under a bridge? How would you survive?

   • Are you persistent? Write about a time when you were persistent and it paid off.

   • Do you think living on your own with no parents telling you to go to school would be simple or difficult? Explain your answer.

   • How much do you depend on your family to provide your basic needs: food, clothing, shelter? Write about each of these needs and how they are met for you.

8. Sequencing: Write the first and last paragraphs from *A Single Shard* on index cards. Then select and copy eight to ten random paragraphs from the middle of the book. Share the cards with students and challenge them to place the cards in sequential order. Guide students to place the first and last paragraphs correctly; don't worry about the middle paragraphs. After they agree on the order, ask students to write paragraphs predicting what the book will be about.

Vocabulary Activities

1. Crossword: Have students create a crossword puzzle with some of the vocabulary words from the book to assess prior knowledge. Helpful hint: when creating crossword puzzles, have students use grid paper first before transferring the puzzles to the computer.

2. Target Word Pictionary®: Have students divide into two teams. Give one person a vocabulary word about which to draw. Artists may not speak while drawing. Have teammates guess the target words. Some suggested words from *A Single Shard* include: scholars (7), gruel (9), brandishing (37), pantaloons (56), surreptitiously (65), guffaw (74), persimmons (109), courtiers (116), donned (126), and medallions (148).

3. Target Word Maps: Have students complete word maps for vocabulary words of a certain part of speech. For example, adverbs from *A Single Shard* would include: precariously (20), surreptitiously (65), fiendishly (82), frenetically (94), absentmindedly (98), grudgingly (104), progressively (106), studiously (112), and stoutly (112).

Word Map for an Adverb

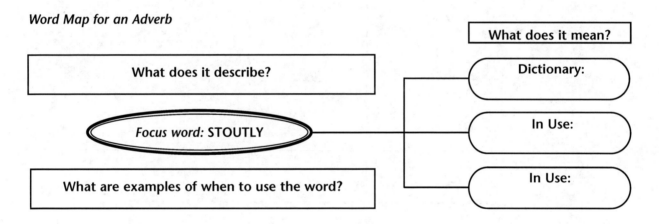

4. Synonym Survival: Have students stand in a circle. Say a recently studied vocabulary word and toss a ball (or other small object) to a student. The student has five seconds to say a synonym for the word given. One point is earned by the class for each correct answer. At the end of one turn, retrieve the ball and start again, saying the word and tossing the ball to another student. Set a time limit and challenge students to earn ten points by the end of the game. This game can be modified by requiring students to give antonyms.

5. Writing Paragraphs: Have students select five to ten vocabulary words and use as many of the words as they can in a summary paragraph about the chapter.

6. Vocabulary Sort: Have students sort vocabulary words into categories (e.g., nouns, verbs, and adjectives/adverbs).

7. Odd One Out: Use vocabulary words from one or two chapters. Have students make a chain of four words. One word in the chain is the vocabulary word, two words are synonyms for the vocabulary word, and one word does not go with the others. (Mix the sequence of the words in the chain.) Students should exchange their chains, underline the word that does not belong with the others, and explain why it does not belong.

8. Vocabulary Boxes: Cut a pattern for a cube (pattern included) from construction paper. Before the cube is glued together, each face should contain one of the following: a vocabulary word, the definition of the word, an illustration of the word, a synonym of the word, an antonym of the word, and a sentence using the word. Display the vocabulary boxes in the room.

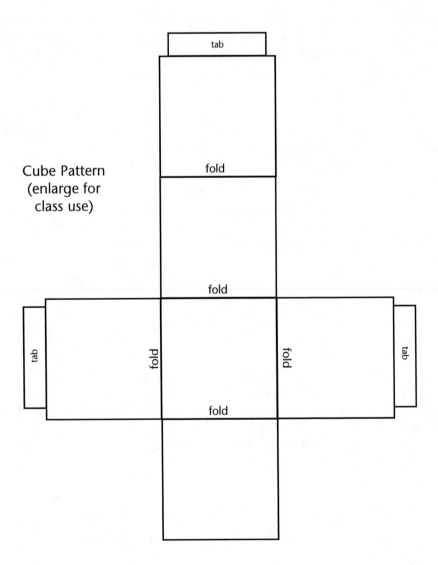

Cube Pattern
(enlarge for
class use)

Using Predictions

We all make predictions as we read—little guesses about what will happen next, how a conflict will be resolved, which details will be important to the plot, which details will help fill in our sense of a character. Students should be encouraged to predict, to make sensible guesses as they read the novel.

As students work on their predictions, these discussion questions can be used to guide them: What are some of the ways to predict? What is the process of a sophisticated reader's thinking and predicting? What clues does an author give to help us make predictions? Why are some predictions more likely to be accurate than others?

Create a chart for recording predictions. This could be either an individual or class activity. As each subsequent chapter is discussed, students can review and correct their previous predictions about plot and characters as necessary.

Use the facts and ideas the author gives.

Use your own prior knowledge.

Apply any new information (i.e., from class discussion) that may cause you to change your mind.

Predictions
_____
_____
_____
_____

Prediction Chart

What characters have we met so far?	What is the conflict in the story?	What are your predictions?	Why did you make those predictions?

Using Character Webs

Attribute webs are simply a visual representation of a character from the novel. They provide a systematic way for students to organize and recap the information they have about a particular character. Attribute webs may be used after reading the novel to recapitulate information about a particular character, or completed gradually as information unfolds. They may be completed individually or as a group project.

One type of character attribute web uses these divisions:

- How a character acts and feels. (How does the character act? How do you think the character feels? How would you feel if this happened to you?)

- How a character looks. (Close your eyes and picture the character. Describe him/her to me.)

- Where a character lives. (Where and at what time does the character live?)

- How others feel about the character. (How does another specific character feel about our character?)

In group discussion about the characters described in student attribute webs, the teacher can ask for backup proof from the novel. Inferential thinking can be included in the discussion.

Attribute webs need not be confined to characters. They may also be used to organize information about a concept, object, or place.

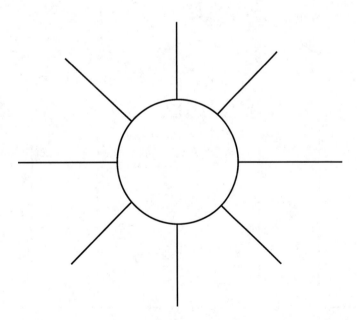

Attribute Boxes

Directions: Record evidence about Tree-ear's character within the other boxes.

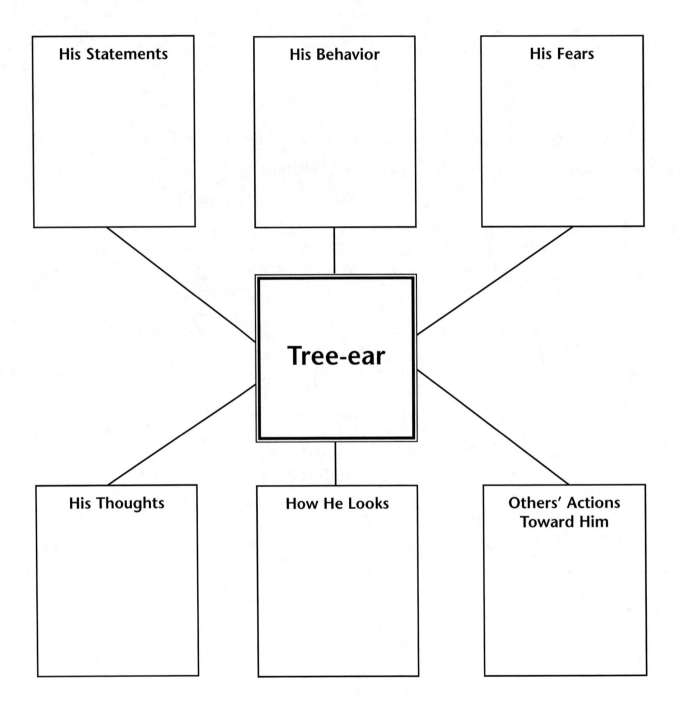

His Statements

His Behavior

His Fears

Tree-ear

His Thoughts

How He Looks

Others' Actions Toward Him

Problem-solving Alternatives Chart

Directions: Tree-ear faces many problems throughout the story. As you read the book, record some of the problems he faces and his solutions. Then record solutions of your own.

Problem	Tree-ear's Solution	Alternative Idea of Your Own

Inference Flow Chart

Directions: Fill in the boxes of the flow chart with the events portrayed in *A Single Shard*. In the ovals beneath, state what emotions and feelings are inferred.

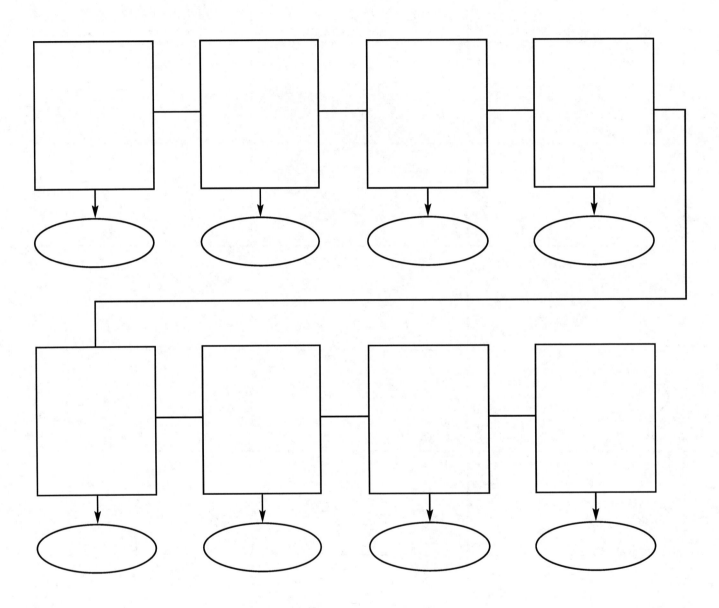

Story Map

Characters_____

_____

Time and Place_____

_____

Problem_____

_____

_____

Goal_____

_____

_____

Beginning ———▶ Development ———▶ Outcome

_____

_____

_____

_____

_____

Resolution_____

_____

_____

_____

Setting

Problem

Goal

Episodes

Resolution

Chapters 1–3

Vocabulary

bulging (3)	protruded (3)	perusal (4)	hoisted (4)
ruefully (5)	complied (5)	scholars (7)	beckoning (8)
gruel (9)	oafish (11)	celadon (12)	emboldened (14)
derision (18)	precariously (20)	wielding (21)	rifle (28)
trundled (31)	impudent (37)	brandishing (37)	

Discussion Questions

1. What is funny about Crane-man's question at the beginning of the book? *(Crane-man and Tree-ear often joke about their poverty. "Have you hungered well today?" is one of their jokes.)*

2. Do you think it is okay for Tree-ear to watch the man losing rice for a few minutes before stopping him? Explain your answer. *(Answers will vary.)*

3. What common phrase do we use today for "good deserves good"? *(One good turn deserves another.)*

4. Why is it important that Crane-man and Tree-ear do not beg for food or clothing? *(Working gives a man dignity where begging does not.)*

5. What does Crane-man mean when he says, "Scholars read the great words of the world. But you and I must learn to read the world itself"? *(Educated people often depend on books for what they know of the world. Crane-man and Tree-ear depend on the sights and sounds around them to learn about the world.)*

6. How does Crane-man's life compare to that of a crane? *(Cranes often stand on one leg and live long lives, and so it is with Crane-man.)*

7. Compare Tree-ear to the rectangular clay box. How are they alike? *(On the outside, Tree-ear appears to be a poor, plain orphan. But on the inside he has brilliant thoughts, ideas, and a great imagination. The box appears plain on the outside, but inside holds the surprise of more boxes fitting neatly inside.)*

8. Why do you think Min's anger loses its edge after Tree-ear explains that stealing would make him no better than a dog? *(Min sees Tree-ear on the inside—that the boy has honor and morals—instead of concentrating on Tree-ear's ragged outward appearance.)*

9. Do you think Tree-ear cries from the pain of the blisters? Explain. *(Answers will vary. Tree-ear cries from exhaustion.)*

10. What process does Crane-man use to clean the wound? Does this surprise you? Explain. *(Crane-man soaks the bandaged wound in the river, removes the soiled wrap, and applies a paste of ground herbs to fight infection.)*

11. Whose fault is it that the wood-gathering chore wasn't completed? What do you think Min and Tree-ear learn from the experience? *(It is Min's fault that the wood was not placed at the*

---

kiln because he wasn't specific in his instructions. Min learns to give better instructions and Tree-ear learns to ask questions.)

12. Why does Crane-man offer to help Tree-ear chop wood? *(He knows Tree-ear's hand will be slow to heal with so much wood chopping.)*

13. Discuss the charity of Kang helping to unload the cart. What does Tree-ear learn about Min during his and Kang's conversation? *(Kang is younger than Min and more able to chop and stack wood. Kang tells Tree-ear that Min has needed help for a while because he can't keep up with his wood chopping duties.)*

14. How are Crane-man and Min's wife compared in the book? *(Both are nice and have gentle eyes.)*

15. Why is Tree-ear excited that he can continue working for Min for no pay? Would you work so hard for no pay? Explain. *(Tree-ear hopes that someday he will be able to sit at the wheel and throw a pot. The only way to do this is to work for Min.)*

16. Why is Tree-ear frustrated with himself when he learns how Crane-man broke his crutch? *(Tree-ear has always been the one to go to the beach when there is a run of flounder. He feels that he has let Crane-man down.)*

17. Crane-man says that it is a waste to spend too much time grieving over what cannot be changed. What does he mean by this? What are other familiar ways to say this? *(He means that when something bad happens, one should move on and not dwell on it. Don't cry over spilled milk. Put your past behind you.)*

Supplementary Activities

1. Research: Have students research the word *jiggeh*. As part of their research, students may examine the cover of the book. Ask: What does the item on Tree-ear's back resemble? Have students research the innovation of the backpack.

2. Creative Writing: Tree-ear knows no family other than Crane-man. Ask students to consider what Tree-ear's family might have been like. Instruct them to create an imaginary family tree for Tree-ear. Students should then draw conclusions as to what trade Tree-ear might have learned from his real father and write a paragraph about this trade.

Chapters 4–6

Vocabulary

fervently (38)	curt (40)	unobtrusive (41)	felicitous (41)
sieving (43)	suffice (43)	vigilance (50)	translucent (51)
rendered (53)	untoward (54)	pantaloons (56)	garb (58)
incising (59)	emissary (61)	impending (65)	surreptitiously (65)
inscribed (67)	clucking (68)	feigning (69)	pretense (70)

Discussion Questions

1. Why does Tree-ear reason with himself about bringing his own bowl? *(He is reassuring himself that he is not stealing. He is simply saving some of his food for Crane-man.)*

2. Why do you think Min's wife teases Tree-ear after he nearly hits her with the bowl? *(She senses his embarrassment and is trying to make him feel better.)*

3. How would you have solved the problem of wild animals eating the leftover food in the bowl? *(Answers will vary.)*

4. Why do you think Min's wife refills the bowl with food after Tree-ear hides it each day? *(Answers will vary. She knows Tree-ear and Crane-man aren't getting enough food and wants them to have more.)*

5. Describe the process of draining the clay. *(The clay is put into shallow holes lined with grasscloth. The clay and water are mixed into mud and then sieved and left for several days for the water to evaporate.)*

6. Why do you think Tree-ear is so timid around Min when he is angry? *(The first time Tree-ear saw Min upset, Min hit him.)*

7. What is the main problem with Min's work? *(He works too slowly.)* Is working slowly necessarily a bad thing? Explain. *(Answers will vary.)*

8. How does Tree-ear's skill of observation help him discover Kang's secret? *(Tree-ear notices Kang going to the kiln with a covered cart. Usually, no one covers a cart of pottery to be fired.)*

9. What do you think about Tree-ear watching Kang all the time? How would you feel if someone were watching you all the time? *(Answers will vary.)*

10. How can a river remind a person of faraway places? *(The water in a river is never still. It flows continuously downstream to faraway places.)*

11. Do you think it is wrong to give away a gift you were given? Explain your answer. *(Answers will vary.)*

12. What laws do we have today that protect people's ideas and intellectual property? *(copyrights, trademarks, registered trademarks)*

13. Why do you think Tree-ear feels ashamed after he substitutes his own clay petal for one of Min's? *(The pot is not his to tamper with and he shouldn't have touched it.)*

14. Have you ever feigned disinterest in something that you were very interested in? Describe the situation and why you pretended not to be interested. *(Answers will vary.)*

15. Why does the emissary suspect that Min created the wine pot used at the previous night's dinner? *(the melon shape, flawless design)*

Supplementary Activities

1. Research/Writing: The author notes that the glaze for the celadon pottery was probably invented by mistake. Ask students, "What other things do we use today that were invented by accident?" Have students research inventions that happened by mistake using the following books: *Accidents May Happen: 50 Inventions Discovered By Mistake* and *Mistakes That Worked*, both by Charlotte Foltz Jones. Have each student choose one item from one of the books and give an oral report about it.

2. Symmetry: The pots that Min threw on the wheel were symmetrical; each side of the pot was identical in shape and size to the opposite side. Have students create a design on one side of a paper and then recreate the design on the other side of the paper. Students may add color to their design so that the colors are symmetrical as well.

3. Research: Have students use library resources and the Internet to research chrysanthemums. What do they look like? Where do they grow? How many different varieties are there? Students should summarize information they uncover in a report. They may include a drawing of a chrysanthemum on the cover page, or a small chrysanthemum formed from modeling clay.

Chapters 7–9

Vocabulary

harangued (73)	guffaw (74)	pliant (75)	dismissively (77)
replicas (79)	fiendishly (82)	placid (84)	suffused (85)
marred (85)	shards (86)	noxious (88)	tumultuous (89)
frenetically (94)	apprentices (96)	absentmindedly (98)	bafflement (101)
stance (102)	grudgingly (104)	inscribed (105)	progressively (106)

Discussion Questions

1. Why do you think Min is so irritable after the emissary's visit? *(He is nervous about creating pottery that might get him the commission.)* Describe a situation when you were nervous about doing something important. *(Answers will vary.)*

2. Why do you think Min chooses not to visit Kang's display that day? *(Answers will vary.)*

3. Why do you think Tree-ear thinks that Min has never laughed? *(Min is always angry and gruff with Tree-ear.)*

4. Tree-ear has drained clay for Min for a while at this point in the story. Describe what you think he feels as he drains the clay and knows it needs one or two more drainings. *(Answers will vary.)*

5. Is there any part of the pottery process that Tree-ear does not enjoy? What parts are his favorites? *(He does not enjoy chopping wood and cutting clay. He does enjoy watching Min when he throws a pot on the wheel and crafts his inlay work.)*

6. What does Tree-ear believe that Min's pottery design could represent for the emissary? *(traditional design and innovative processes)*

7. Describe the firing process of the pottery. *(The pieces are loaded into the kiln and placed on seashells. Wood is stacked carefully and fires are lit inside the kiln. Then the door is closed. Wood is added through holes in the kiln walls until the potter believes the correct temperature has been reached, then the holes are sealed until the fire burns out.)*

8. Do you think Crane-man has really become fat and lazy? Explain your answer. *(Answers will vary.)*

9. Retell the story of how Crane-man came to live under the bridge. *(When Crane-man was on his way to live with the monks, he came upon a fox. He was scared and went to sleep under the bridge for the night. He never made it to the temple.)*

10. Why is Emissary Kim still interested in Min's work? *(He is interested because Min's quality is far superior to Kang's work.)*

11. Why do you think Min chooses to wave off the offer of a chance at a commission instead of showing some of the shards of the inlay work he destroyed? *(He is ashamed of the staining that took place and will only show work that is perfect.)*

12. Which favor do you think is greatest: Min feeding Tree-ear 1 1/2 meals per work day or Tree-ear journeying to Songdo to take Min's work to the emissary? Explain your answer. *(Answers will vary.)*

13. Why do you think Tree-ear hesitates to tell Crane-man about his trip? *(He is afraid to talk about the trip because the idea is still frightening to him.)*

14. How does Tree-ear feel about the news that he will never make a pot? Refer to examples from the text. *(He is disappointed and ashamed to be an orphan. He can't understand why it makes a difference whether he is Min's son or not.)*

15. What does Crane-man mean when he says, "My friend, the same wind that blows one door shut often blows another open"? *(He means that the loss of one opportunity may lead to the gain of another.)*

16. Why does Crane-man refuse to live at Ajima's house while Tree-ear is away? *(Crane-man is too proud to accept handouts.)*

17. Why do you think Tree-ear makes a clay monkey for Crane-man? *(Crane-man often calls Tree-ear "monkey" out of affection. It is a logical choice.)*

Supplementary Activities

1. Research/Science: Have students find pictures of lotus blossoms and peonies on the Internet or in a book. They should answer the following questions: Where do these plants grow? What other flowers do they resemble? If resources are available, purchase some flower seeds. Have students work a flower garden plot of their own.

2. Creative Writing: Have students write a story about how the fox got the reputation of being "fiendishly clever." Students should be prepared to share their story with the class.

3. Research/History: As a class, research apprentices and trades that were practiced long ago. Have each student choose one trade to research in depth. Students should then create a skit to show the class how the trade was done.

Chapters 10–11

Vocabulary

flinched (109)	persimmons (109)	trepidation (109)	studiously (112)
stoutly (112)	courtiers (116)	embers (117)	thatched (117)
plying (118)	impeccable (119)	quell (121)	menacing (122)
pallor (122)	pinioned (123)	desperation (125)	donned (126)
heedless (127)			

Discussion Questions

1. Why do you think Tree-ear keeps track of the days he travels? *(It is a way to help him bring closure to another successful travel day.)*

2. Why does the author describe Tree-ear's sleeping on the *jiggeh* as "a welcome reminder of his duty"? *(Tree-ear is on a mission to deliver the vases safely to the palace in Songdo. The* jiggeh *is kept close to him so nothing will happen to it.)*

3. Describe how Tree-ear decides what to mold with his piece of clay each day. *(He simply molds and shapes the clay until a figure emerges.)*

4. According to Crane-man, how are fire and falling water alike? *(They are always the same, yet always changing.)* Are people like fire and water? Explain your answer. *(Answers will vary.)*

5. Tree-ear and Crane-man's fear of foxes could be characterized as superstitious. How do you think superstitions were started? *(People told stories to explain the things they didn't understand. People naturally fear what they can't understand.)*

6. Describe one thing you are afraid of because you do not know about it. *(Answers will vary.)*

7. What is the significance of Tree-ear's discovery that Kang's design had already been copied in Puyo? *(It means that others will be doing the same inlay work and there will be more competition with Min.)*

8. What clues does Tree-ear have that the man at the Rock of the Falling Flowers is bad? *(The stranger is rude in his response to Tree-ear's question. He is oddly pale and unkempt. His smile isn't genuine.)*

9. How does his hard work for Min help Tree-ear in his battle against the robber? *(He is stronger and stands his ground.)*

10. Why does Tree-ear consider what it would be like to leap from the cliff like the women who leapt before him? *(He is ashamed of not completing the task he set out to do and doesn't want to tell anyone that he has failed.)*

11. Do you think Tree-ear really believes it is likely that the second vase lay unbroken at the base of the cliff? Why or why not? *(Answers will vary.)*

12. How does Tree-ear come up with the idea of taking a shard of the pottery to the emissary? *(He recalls his idea from when the emissary visited Min after the destruction of the first set of pots.)*

Supplementary Activities

1. Creative Writing: Have students write a story about traveling on foot through an unfamiliar country. What dangers would one face? What kinds of things might one discover? Would people be as friendly to weary travelers as they were in this book? Students should be prepared to share their story with the class.

2. Climate/Research: Ask a group of students to research the climate of Korea to determine what month Tree-ear traveled to Songdo. The students should write a report using the information they uncovered to support the estimated dates of travel. Have students share their report with the rest of the class.

3. Creative Writing: Instruct each student to choose a familiar landmark in the area and write a story about it. The story should be similar to Crane-man's story about the Rock of the Falling Flowers. It should represent the history of the area and have a good ending that teaches some kind of lesson. Students should be prepared to share their story with the class.

Chapters 12–13

Vocabulary

crooning (132)	behalf (133)	nudge (134)	anxiety (134)
gestured (135)	characters (136)	incredulous (136)	brazen (136)
chastened (136)	skepticism (138)	clarity (138)	scampered (141)
jostled (142)	barrage (144)	eddy (145)	groped (147)
intricate (148)	medallions (148)		

Discussion Questions

1. Why does Tree-ear continue his journey in such earnest? *(He is determined to complete his mission without further delay.)*

2. Why do you think Tree-ear has such a poor self-image? *(He has been a poor orphan all of his life and is used to people looking down on him.)*

3. What clues are given about Tree-ear's love for pottery once he steps inside the palace walls? *(He stops and marvels at the ceramic roof tiles that were crafted in Ch'ulp'o years ago.)*

4. What emotion do you sense when someone folds his or her arms when looking at you? *(Answers will vary; irritation, anger, etc.)*

5. Why does the shard give Tree-ear the courage to continue talking to the emissary? (*The shard still shows the intricate inlay work as well as the flawless design of the pottery.*)

6. Why do you think Emissary Kim's assistant is so skeptical about rewarding Min a commission? (*He thinks it is necessary to see an entire piece of work in order to award a commission.*)

7. Why do you think the emissary shows kindness toward Tree-ear? (*He is sorry that Tree-ear was robbed and grateful that Tree-ear continued his journey to the palace. The emissary also wants Tree-ear to be safe on his journey home to tell his master of the commission.*)

8. Describe a time when you were so thankful you were at a loss for words. (*Answers will vary.*)

9. What decision do you think Ajima makes while she is talking to Tree-ear? (*She decides to let Min tell Tree-ear about Crane-man's death.*)

10. What do you think Min is looking at over Tree-ear's shoulder? (*Answers will vary. He is watching Ajima coming down the path.*)

11. Why does Tree-ear think he is hearing things when Min says Tree-ear's work is good? (*He has just heard about Crane-man's death and isn't thinking clearly.*)

12. Do you think it would have made any difference if Tree-ear had been in Ch'ulp'o when Crane-man fell from the bridge? Would Tree-ear have been able to save him? Cite references from the book to explain your answer. (*Tree-ear would most likely have been working at Min's and would not have been at the bridge at the time of the accident. He would not have been able to help.*)

13. What do we learn about Tree-ear's religious beliefs after Crane-man's death? (*He believes that Crane-man has gone to an afterlife where he will travel on two good legs.*)

14. Why do you think Min and Ajima offer to take Tree-ear in after Crane-man's death? (*He is an orphan and has no place to turn. He wants to learn to throw pots and Min has been offered a commission and needs the help. They also miss their son who died.*)

15. What advice does Tree-ear recall as he is feeling overwhelmed and thinking about the pot he wants to make? What does it mean? (*"One hill, one valley." It means to take everything one day at a time.*)

Supplementary Activities

1. Research/Geography: As a class, use maps, books, and the Internet to research the rivers in Korea. On page 151 the author provides information about Tree-ear's journey to Songdo. Using the maps and the information on page 151, try to determine the path of Tree-ear's journey and mark it on a map. Mark the path that took Tree-ear home by ocean.

2. Research/Science: Have students research the various ways scientists determine the ages of trees. As an experiment, estimate the girth of a man's body using a piece of string. Using the information gathered about tree size and its relationship to the age of the tree, estimate the age of a tree that measures the size of the girth of a man. Have students use information from their research to support the findings of the experiment.

Post-reading Discussion Questions

1. How might things have been different if Tree-ear had lived at the temple with the monks instead of with Crane-man?

2. What does Tree-ear learn about patience and hard work?

3. How do you think Tree-ear felt as he went to visit his old home under the bridge one last time?

4. How believable was the book *A Single Shard*? Do you think the events in this story could have happened? Explain your answer.

5. Have you read a story similar to this one? How is it the same? How is it different?

6. When you want a job, you have to "sell yourself" to an employer. How did Tree-ear sell himself to Min?

7. Throughout the book, Tree-ear recalls many things Crane-man taught him. Was Crane-man a wise man? Why or why not?

8. Tree-ear traveled a great distance by himself to deliver the pottery to the emissary. What were some of the dangers he encountered during his journey? How would his journey be different today?

9. Tree-ear spent a lot of time in the book eavesdropping and spying on people. What do you think of this kind of behavior?

10. Why do you think Min was so harsh with Tree-ear? Explain your answer.

11. How does this book help you realize all you have to be thankful for?

12. Is *A Single Shard* a good title for the book? Explain your answer.

Post-reading Extension Activities

1. Choose one piece of advice recalled by Tree-ear in the book and write a composition about what it means and how it will affect the choices you make in the future.

2. Write a poem about life from Crane-man's point of view.

3. Create a Venn diagram comparing life in 12th-century Korea to life today. How are our lives alike and different?

4. The author developed the story for this book based on a single piece of pottery in Korea. Develop an outline of another story that could have been written using the same piece of pottery described on page 148 of the book.

5. Select one chapter from the book to dramatize. Create a script, cast parts, and arrange for props. Present your play to the class.

6. Develop an outline for a sequel to *A Single Shard*. Remember to include a list of characters, setting, plot, problems, climax, and resolutions.

7. Compare *A Single Shard* to other stories you have read about a character from a different century, such as *Catherine Called Birdy, The Whipping Boy,* or *The Midwife's Apprentice.*

8. Write a commercial to advertise the book as a movie. This is called a trailer. Record your trailer in an announcer's voice on a tape recorder. Remember, don't tell everything that happens in the book.

9. Write an acrostic poem about one of the characters in the book.

   Example:

   Meticulous in his work, Min carefully
   Inspects every piece of pottery he creates.
   Notorious for being slowly made and expensive, Min's pottery is coveted by many.

10. Using magazines, pictures, or words, create a collage of the emotions of the characters. Search for pictures of faces that best summarize the emotions felt in each chapter. Write an essay describing the collage and the feelings represented.

11. Write about how the book would have been different if Min's trade had been basket weaving or fishing.

Assessment for *A Single Shard*

Assessment is an ongoing process. The following ten items can be completed during the novel study. Once finished, the student and teacher will check the work. Points may be added to indicate the level of understanding.

Name _____ Date _____

Student   **Teacher**

_____   _____   1. Write a conversation that Tree-ear might have with the emissary as he delivers the first pottery from Min's commission.

_____   _____   2. Describe the events of one conflict that happened in *A Single Shard*. List different ways the main character could have solved the conflict.

_____   _____   3. Write a letter or e-mail to Linda Sue Park telling her whether or not you enjoyed the book.

_____   _____   4. What if Ajima and Min hadn't invited Tree-ear to become a part of their family? Create a detailed outline of events that could have taken place through the rest of winter and into spring. Be sure to include new challenges Tree-ear would have faced living on his own under the bridge.

_____   _____   5. Discuss the post-reading discussion questions on page 22 of this guide with partner. Choose one question to answer in a multi-paragraph essay.

_____   _____   6. Create a flow chart of events in the book's plot.

_____   _____   7. What was the climax of the book? Write a persuasive composition stating what you believe was the climax of the book. Cite specific quotes from the book to support your answer.

_____   _____   8. Research and write an essay about the creation of handmade pottery today. How is the process alike and different from that used in the 12th century? Cite references from books and the Internet as you write.

_____   _____   9. Choose one of the extension activities (page 23 of this guide) to complete.

_____   _____   10. What was the significance of the ceramic monkey in the story? Write an essay citing references from the book explaining its significance.